The TimeOut Papers

THE TIMEOUT PAPERS

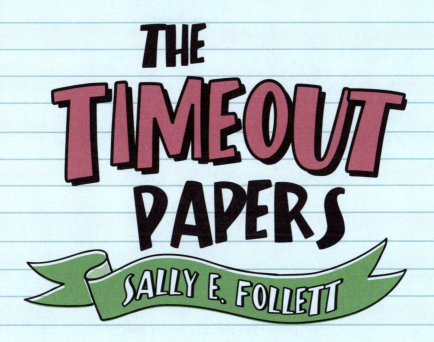

SALLY E. FOLLETT

TEACHING CHILDREN TO LEARN AND GROW FROM THEIR MISTAKES

SOPHIA INSTITUTE PRESS
Manchester, New Hampshire

Sophia Institute Press
Box 5284, Manchester, NH 03108
1-800-888-9344

www.SophiaInstitute.com

Sophia Institute Press® is a registered trademark of Sophia Institute.

Paperback ISBN 978-1-64413-247-0

eBook ISBN 978-1-64413-248-7

Library of Congress Control Number: 2020942099

First printing

*In thanksgiving to God for the gifts of
Ethan, Isaac, Emma, and Simon*

TIME TO REWARD 87

NOTE

FROM THE AUTHOR

Dear Sisters and Brothers in Christ,

Training children in the way they should go is a journey of many adjectives. For many, including me, this joyful, blessed journey is riddled with frustration, moods, unkind words, actions, and doubts. When my two oldest children were eight and seven, sitting for a timeout just wasn't enough. I knew they knew better than to do what they did at times!

The Holy Spirit, thankfully, planted a seed that has grown into a volume of subjects that we all face in raising children. Instead of riding the tide of frustration, one day I paused and said a prayer. Then, with the help of Our Good Lord, I sat down and wrote a paper and asked my child to copy it for his punishment. It was gentle and contained a prayer. A light was turned on for me that day as I discovered a new, peaceful way to train my children. Frustration met hope, and many papers have since been penned.

In the beginning, I shared copies of the papers with my friends because a light is not meant to be put under a basket. I wondered if one day they could be shared in a book. With the great help of Sophia Institute Press, the result of that wonder has found a way to your home.

In speaking of the Gentiles in his letter to the Romans, Saint Paul explains why mercy and gentleness are encouraged in using *The TimeOut Papers*, for he teaches, "Just as you were once disobedient to God but now have received mercy because of their disobedience, so they have now been disobedient in order that by the mercy shown to you they also may receive mercy. For God has consigned all men to disobedience, that he may have mercy upon all" (11:30–32).

Stumbling upon that verse was an eye opener, and it came to me at a very providential time. My prayer is that your children grow in virtue and love of neighbor and that the peace of Christ be alive in your home. May God's mercy be upon you, and may He bless your family.

Sally E. Follett

The TimeOut Papers

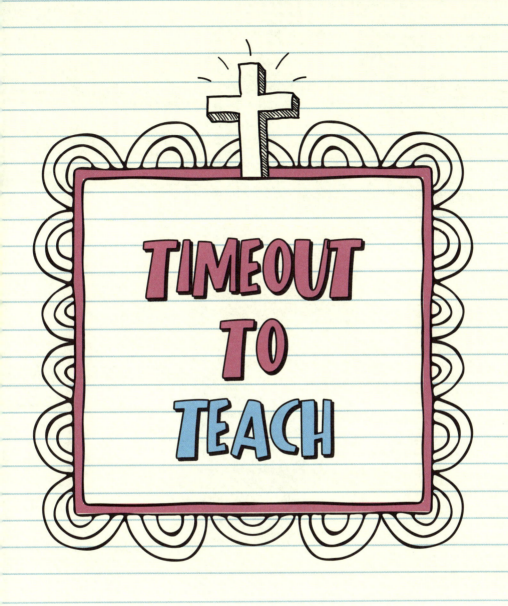

TIMEOUT TO TEACH

The papers in this section are meant to be read aloud, at least the first time. As you read, younger children should repeat each line after you. A good reader could simply read the paper aloud. If an older child who knows better commits a fault, consider having the child copy the paper. Please note that the Scripture verse is not meant to be part of the child's copywork. Be gentle, and give your child time to think. Trust that the Holy Spirit is at work.

Later, when peace has returned, consider gently asking the older child about what was learned in timeout. The insights my children gained often showed me how the Holy Spirit worked during timeout, and this gave me a greater trust in God.

WHAT IS A VIRTUE?

A virtue is a good habit by which we act uprightly over and over again with God's help. Being virtuous means trying really hard to do what is right and saying no to what is wrong.

❧

Dear Jesus, I want to be good and righteous, so please help me. Amen.

Make every effort to supplement your faith with virtue, and virtue with knowledge, and knowledge with self-control, and self-control with steadfastness, and steadfastness with godliness, and godliness with brotherly affection, and brotherly affection with love. (2 Peter 1:5–7)

WHAT IS A SIN?

Saint Augustine taught that a sin is something said, done, or desired contrary to the eternal law of God. If we are sorry for our sins and try to make things right, we stay connected to God and our neighbors.

Dear God, I belong to You, and I want to be good. Please teach me to say no to what is wrong. Amen.

By rejecting conscience, certain persons have made shipwreck of their faith. (1 Timothy 1:19)

DRAWING ON THE WALLS

Drawing on paper is good. Drawing on the walls, the floor, or the furniture damages something of value. And the damage must be repaired.

❧

Dear Jesus, help me do something nice to make up for what I've done. Help me say "I'm sorry" too. Amen.

The Lord disciplines him whom he loves. (Hebrews 12:6)

NOT PICKING UP MY TOYS

Why do I resist picking up my toys? If I pick them up, then everything will be all neat before bed. No one will step on toys in the dark. Tomorrow, I will have fun taking them all out again!

❧

Dear God, help me be kind and pick up my toys with joy to show that I love my family. Amen.

But all things should be done decently and in order. (1 Corinthians 14:40)

HAVING A BAD DAY: TIME TO PRAY

It seems as though nothing is
going right for me today.

*Dear Jesus, please show me the
way. Help me to be good and forgive
others. Lift up my soul and help
me feel happy again. Amen.*

*The LORD is near to the
brokenhearted, and saves the
crushed in spirit. (Psalm 34:18)*

POUTING

Why do I pout? Why are my feelings
so strong that they overpower me?

෧✐

*O Jesus, help me stop feeling sorry
for myself. Teach me to lay down
my selfish feelings, forgive others,
and move forward. Amen.*

*I can do all things in him who
strengthens me. (Philippians 4:13)*

WHINING

Whining sounds awful and does not receive a reward. I must choose to be pleasant even when I don't get my way. Then the virtue of goodness will be with me.

Dear God, help me accept with decency when I don't get my request. Love,

Do all things without grumbling or questioning, that you may be blameless and innocent, children of God. (Philippians 2:14–15)

SCREAMING

Screaming hurts people's ears and takes peace away. Well-thought words are a better way to communicate that I'm upset. Screaming is for danger and outdoor sports.

Dear Jesus, help me use good words and a good tone of voice. Amen.

And let the peace of Christ rule in your hearts. (Colossians 3:15)

TATTLING

Tattling means telling on another before that person has a chance to tell on himself or herself. I should encourage wrongdoers to admit what they did and pray for them to be truthful and have courage.

Dear God, help me to be a good friend. Amen.
(I might need to tell on a person who won't tell on himself. Dear God, help Mom and Dad explain this to me.)

But he who restrains his lips is prudent. (Proverbs 10:19)

CALLING NAMES

When I call someone a bad name, I hurt that person and smudge my character. The Golden Rule reminds us to treat others as we would want to be treated.

Dear Jesus, help me do a charitable act for _____, whom I offended. Please forgive me. Love,

So whatever you wish that men would do to you, do so to them; for this is the law and the prophets. (Matthew 7:12)

FLUSHING THE WRONG THINGS

If I flush something good, it will never come back. If I flush something that doesn't belong in the toilet, my parents may have to hire a plumber to unplug the pipes.

Dear Jesus, help me to respect our home. Love,

Show yourself in all respects a model of good deeds. (Titus 2:7)

LEAVING A MESS IN THE BATHROOM

I should wipe the toilet and sink clean before I leave the bathroom. It is kind to clean up after myself.

Dear Jesus, help me make the bathroom nice for the next person every time. Amen.

Little children, let us not love in word or speech but in deed and truth. (1 John 3:18)

LEAVING THE OUTSIDE DOOR OPEN

When I leave the outside door open, heat or cool air leaves the house and insects come in. Heating and cooling our home costs money and uses the earth's resources.

❧

Dear Jesus, help me take time to close the door. Amen.

The fruit of the spirit is love, joy, peace, patience, kindness, goodness, faithfulness, gentleness, self-control. (Galatians 5:22–23)

SLAMMING THE DOOR

When I slam the door, I take peace away from others. Closing a door gently is an act of kindness, and it helps the door last longer too!

~∽◈

Dear Jesus, let there be peace on earth, and let it begin with me! Amen.

Blessed are the peacemakers, for they shall be called sons of God. (Matthew 5:9)

LEAVING LIGHTS ON UNNECESSARILY

When I turn off unnecessary lights,
I help our family conserve money
and the earth's resources.

*Dear Jesus, teach me to turn off
the lights when I leave a room.
Thank you for the sun! Amen.*

*God made the two great lights,
the greater to rule the day and the
lesser to rule the night; he made
the stars also. (Genesis 1:16)*

LEAVING SHOES AND SOCKS AROUND THE HOUSE

Leaving shoes and socks lying around makes our house messy. A tidy house is more open to welcoming guests and is a good reflection on our family.

❧

Dear Jesus, help me prove that I am big enough to clean up after myself. Amen.

Practice hospitality ungrudgingly to one another. (1 Peter 4:9)

LEAVING THE DINNER TABLE BEFORE BEING EXCUSED

When I ask to be excused from the dinner table, I show respect and humility that has eternal rewards.

❧

Dear Jesus, and my Guardian Angel, help me request to be excused. Love,

The reward for humility and fear of the LORD is riches and honor and life. (Proverbs 22:4)

REJECTING THE FOOD PROVIDED

When I eat food that I don't like, I am acting in a virtue that stores its reward in Heaven. I also show gratitude to those who provided the food.

Dear Jesus, help me smile and be thankful for the things I secretly don't like. Love,

Do not be anxious about your life, what you shall eat or what you shall drink, nor about your body, what you shall put on. (Matthew 6:25)

OVEREATING

St. John Cassian tells us that eating too much, or too soon, or in too picky a manner, can lead to the sin of gluttony.

༄

O Lord, give me the strength of self-control. Teach me to eat responsibly. Love,

Fear not, for I am with you,
be not dismayed, for I am your God;
I will strengthen you, I will help you,
I will uphold you with my victorious
right hand. (Isaiah 41:10)

SNEAKING FOOD

If I am hungry, I should ask permission to have a snack. Eating too often is a habit that leads to obesity, and my parents are protecting me from that vice by making rules that I must honor.

Dear Jesus, help me respect my parents and my body. Amen

Put on the Lord Jesus Christ, and make no provision for the flesh, to gratify its desires. (Romans 13:14)

REFUSING TO SHARE

When I refuse to share, I am not generous. Generosity is a beautiful virtue that shows love. I should share what I have with a good heart.

Dear Jesus, train me to be generous by giving me opportunities to share my riches. Amen.

Give to him who begs from you, and do not refuse him who would borrow from you. (Matthew 5:42)

THROWING AWAY USEFUL THINGS

I should donate the good things I no longer want. Otherwise I show God that I am not thankful for all the good things He has given me.

୧⁄ა

Dear God, I'm sorry for throwing away something useful. Amen.

He who is kind to the poor lends to the LORD, and he will repay him for his deed. (Proverbs 19:17)

COMPLETING HOMEWORK IS A PRIORITY

Homework helps me practice and remember what I have learned. Homework lets my teachers know if I understand what has been taught. Homework isn't fun, but it needs to be done!

Dear God, help me to persevere in my homework! Amen.

Whatever you do ... do all for the glory of God. (1 Corinthians 10:31)

DOING CHORES IS FOR EVERYONE

Family life is like being on a team, on which everyone must do a part. Doing work with joy is a virtue and builds character.

❧

Dear God, help me discover joy in work! Love,

Whatever your task, work heartily, as serving the Lord and not men, knowing that from the Lord you will receive the inheritance as your reward; you are serving the Lord Christ. (Colossians 3:23–24)

FEELING MAD OR BITTER

When I feel hurt by another, I need to forgive quickly and let Jesus do the rest. Forgiveness helps me feel healthy in mind, body, and soul. Forgiveness lays my hurts at the foot of the Cross, and Jesus takes them.

❧

In the name of Jesus I forgive
_____ *for*
_____. *Amen.*

For if you forgive men their trespasses, your heavenly Father also will forgive you. (Matthew 6:14)

FINDING IT DIFFICULT TO FORGIVE OTHERS

Being able to forgive is a gift that must be learned with the tender love of God. I can forgive anything by asking God's grace and then I will feel better.

෬

Dear Jesus, help me to forgive _____ *for* _____. *Amen*

Judge not, and you will not be judged; condemn not, and you will not be condemned; forgive, and you will be forgiven. (Luke 6:37)

HURTING ANOTHER

When I hit, kick, bite, or scratch someone, I damage my relationship with that person, with God, and with anyone else who loves the person I hurt.

❧

Dear Jesus, help me repair my relationship with _____. I am sorry; please forgive me. Amen.

Repay no one evil for evil, but take thought for what is noble in the sight of all. If possible, so far as it depends upon you, live peaceably with all. (Romans 12:17–18)

SAYING "I HATE YOU"

To hate breaks the commandment "Thou shall not kill"; therefore, saying "I hate you" is a serious sin of one's words. Forgiving others allows Jesus to heal my heart and brings me peace.

℮⦿

In the name of Jesus, I forgive _____ for _____. Amen.

If anyone says, "I love God," and hates his brother, he is a liar; for he who does not love his brother whom he has seen, cannot love God whom he has not seen. (1 John 4:20)

MAKING MOM CRY

Sometimes in life we are tempted and do the unthinkable. Turning to Jesus is the key to know what to do next.

ॐ

Dear Jesus, I am so sorry for
_____. *Will You please show me how to make Mom happy again? Amen.*

Love covers a multitude
of sins. (1 Peter 4:8)

GOSSIPING

When I gossip, I hurt another's reputation. The Golden Rule says: do to others as I would have them do to me. Would I want my reputation hurt? No! So I should never gossip about others.

Dear God, please bless _____, whom I hurt. Help me do an act of kindness for _____. Amen.

A whisperer separates close friends. (Proverbs 16:28)

BEING A SPOILSPORT

When an outing or event is planned,
I should try really hard to embrace
it, even if I don't want to do it. This
is a saintly form of selflessness.

*Dear Jesus, help my soul to grow, so I can
be joyful even doing things I don't want
to do. I want to be a good sport. Amen.*

*And he said to all, "If any man
would come after me, let him
deny himself." (Luke 9:23–24)*

BEING LATE

When I'm late, planned activities are disrupted. But being on time is an act of goodness. I must consider how I can improve my planning, so I can be on time.

Dear Jesus, help me strive to be timely—even early! Love,

Look carefully then how you walk, not as unwise men but as wise, making the most of the time. (Ephesians 5:15–16)

COMPLAINING ABOUT GOING TO CHURCH

We must keep holy the Lord's Day; that is one of God's commandments. We go to God's house on earth to worship Him and receive the life of Jesus in the breaking of the bread.

Dear God, I want to stay in communion with you! Help me go to church joyfully, to show you that I'm happy to be Your child.

Remember the sabbath day, to keep it holy. (Exodus 20:8)

BEING LAZY

Being a good worker protects against the sin of sloth. Work brings satisfaction and contributes to the family. Even Jesus was a hard-working carpenter!

❧

Dear Jesus, plant in me the desire to work and be diligent. Love,

The hand of the diligent will rule, while the slothful will be put to forced labor. (Proverbs 12:24)

GETTING UP ON TIME

Setting my alarm and getting up on time is one of the most important things I'll ever learn to do! Whether or not I'm good at this will affect my whole life. Furthermore, if I rise and pray just after my alarm sounds, my day will have a perfect start!

Dear Jesus, remind me to set my alarm, get up when it sounds, and start my day with You. Amen.

For you are all sons of light and sons of the day; we are not of the night or of darkness. So then let us not sleep as others do, but let us keep awake, and be sober. (1 Thessalonians 5:5–6)

INTERRUPTING OTHERS

It is a common courtesy to wait until others have finished speaking before adding to the conversation. When I listen fully, I show respect. When I get excited and interrupt, I show rudeness. I must wait for my turn to speak.

Dear Guardian Angel, please help me wait my turn to speak!

Know this, my beloved brethren, Let every man be quick to hear, slow to speak, slow to anger. (James 1:19)

TAKING MORE THAN MY FAIR SHARE

When I take more than my fair share, it means that someone will not get any. I should take note of how much is left and how many people need to be served after me. It's an act of charity to take just a little.

❧

Dear God, help me think of others first and myself last. Amen.

Let each of you look not only to his own interests, but also to the interests of others. (Philippians 2:4)

BEING PRIDEFUL

Humility is the crown of all virtues.
It means that whatever I have,
whether wealth, wisdom, talents,
or position, I realize these are from
God and He expects me to use
these gifts to serve others and
have a modest view of myself.

*Dear God, help me to grow in humility.
How shall I serve others? Love,*

*When pride comes, then comes
disgrace; but with the humble
is wisdom. (Proverbs 11:2)*

BOASTING

I should resist boasting because boasting isn't appealing to others. I must be careful in how I speak of my talents, giving credit not to myself but to God's goodness.

༒

Dear God, help me use my words to build up others, not myself. Amen.

Let another praise you, and not your own mouth; a stranger, and not your own lips. (Proverbs 27:2)

INSISTING ON EXPENSIVE THINGS

I should not insist on having expensive things. St. Teresa of Calcutta taught something wise. If we spend less on ourselves, we will have something left over to help the poor. Helping others is the true meaning of love.

❧

Dear God, help me desire less for myself, so others can have enough. Amen.

For the poor will never cease out of the land; therefore, I command you, You shall open wide your hand to your brother, to the needy and to the poor, in the land. (Deuteronomy 15:11)

RUINING MY CLOTHES CARELESSLY

I should be thoughtful about all my actions. Ruining my clothing out of carelessness shows my parents that I'm not thankful for what they provide.

Dear God, I'm sorry. Help me think my actions through so I can avoid mistakes. Amen.

If you have not been faithful in the unrighteous [wealth], who will entrust to you the true riches? (Luke 16:11)

DRESSING IMMODESTLY

Modesty means that we should desire decency and cover that which should remain hidden. By dressing modestly, I will protect others from the sin of lust.

☙

Dear God, help me remember to follow our family values and dress decently. Amen.

Women should adorn themselves modestly. (1 Timothy 2:9)

SAYING "THANK YOU"

If I forget to say "thank you," I hurt the feelings of the person who helped me or served me or gave me a gift. Gratitude shows holiness and goodness.

☙

Dear God, please help me say "thank you," even when I don't like what has been given to me. Amen.

Give thanks in all circumstances.
(1 Thessalonians 5:18)

BEING THANKFUL!

Being thankful is the best way
to stay happy. Saying "thank
you" makes others happy.

༄

Dear God, thank You for special treats,
sunshine, nature's beauty, Mom, Dad,
hugs, my hands, and _____.

O give thanks to the LORD, call on
his name, make known his deeds
among the peoples! (Psalm 105:1)

LACKING GRATITUDE

When I'm feeling like all my thoughts are of a selfish nature, I'm probably unhappy. It is uplifting and helpful to think of things I'm grateful for—lots of things!

☙

Dear Jesus, I give You my sadness and beg You to replace it with faith and thanksgiving. Love,

Have no anxiety about anything, but in everything by prayer and [asking] with thanksgiving let your requests be made known to God. And the peace of God, which passes all understanding, will keep your hearts and your minds in Christ Jesus. (Philippians 4:6–7)

PUTTING OTHERS' NEEDS FIRST

When we consider the needs of others, we are being like Jesus. Letting someone have the last slice of pizza makes our soul brighter. Helping Dad even in a small way, such as by waiting patiently, makes God smile. When we let go of our selfish wishes, we are storing up treasure in Heaven!

Dear Jesus, help me to consider others before myself. Amen.

Let no one seek his own good, but the good of his neighbor. (1 Corinthians 10:24)

HELPING MY NEIGHBOR

Love isn't just a feeling. To love means to do things for others with joy. When I help anyone, I am loving. When I love, my soul grows. My soul has the capacity to grow so much that I could be a living saint on earth!

O Lord, help me desire to put love into action. Amen.

This is my commandment, that you love one another as I have loved you. Greater love has no man than this, that a man lay down his life for his friends. (John 15:12–13)

BEING RIGHTEOUS

How can I be good all the time? By always doing the next right thing! A well-lived life is made of millions of little decisions, made well, with God's help. x (

O God, I will try to be righteous. And when I fail, I will pray and try again, and again. Amen. x3

O that you had hearkened to my commandments! Then your peace would have been like a river, and your righteousness like the waves of the sea. (Isaiah 48:18)

NEEDING A PRAYER LIFE

When I spend time with my friends, I get to know them better. It is like that with God too. When I tell God what I care about, He hears me. He can make me feel better and bring me peace and joy. God can give me the gift of faith and help my soul grow closer to Him.

Dear God, I want to know You more. I praise You for Your many gifts. I lay at Your feet the things that hurt me. Thank You for loving me and making my soul long for You. I am Yours. Amen.

Call to me and I will answer you, and will tell you great and hidden things which you have not known. (Jeremiah 33:3)

BREAKING MUNICIPAL LAWS

Laws are in place to keep people safe and make things fair. I need to obey signs, or I could cause an accident. If I break a law, my parents could be charged a fine since I am a minor. When I obey laws, I am a respectable citizen.

Dear God, I am sorry that I broke the law. Help me to honor my family name. Love,

Let every person be subject to the governing authorities. (Romans 13:1)

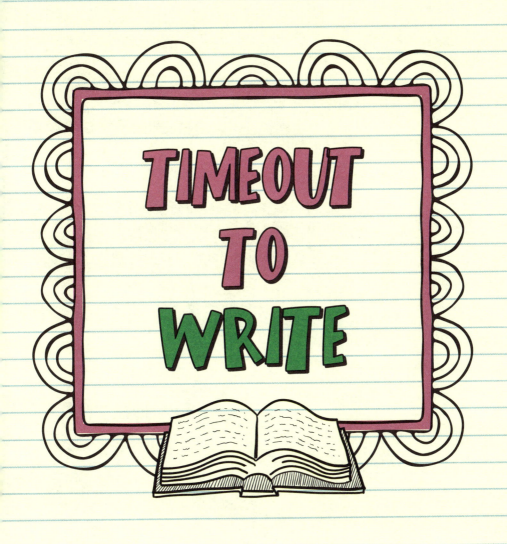

TIMEOUT TO WRITE

Graver actions have stronger consequences. Papers in this section are meant for children who are about eight or older whose consciences are working well and who have fallen to temptation. Handwriting or typing the papers will help children learn to read, write, and spell and give them quiet time for the teaching and the prayer to sink in. The Scripture verses support the teachings, but they are not meant to be copied by the child.

Be kind yet firm in delivering the news that your child must write a paper. If a child refuses to write the paper, smile and tell the child that he or she must forgo some privilege (let the child know which one) until the paper is written.

Pray and trust that the Holy Spirit will move your children's souls in a positive way, so they will see more clearly the extent of their actions.

Papers in this section can also be read aloud to younger children, who can repeat them line by line, per your discretion.

Dear parents, some papers in this section concern use of computers and other such devices. Be aware that many devices offer parental controls, giving you the ability to approve apps, maturity levels, and time limits. You can turn off your child's app functions and Internet usage at any time, remotely, using your phone! Choose a phone for your child that has functions that allow you to control what your child sees and how he or she uses the phone.

LYING

When I lie, it not only hurts my soul; it also makes me lose the trust of others. Deliberately lying is a grave sin that I must resist.

Dear God, give me the courage to tell the truth even when it means I will be punished. Amen.

Truthful lips endure for ever, but a lying tongue is but for a moment. (Proverbs 12:19)

CHEATING

I didn't listen to my conscience, and I cheated. This was a wrong use of my free will, and I have lost the trust of others.

Dear Jesus, I feel terrible. I am sorry. Please forgive me and help me to pick myself up and do some good things to regain other people's trust.

If we confess our sins, he is faithful and just, and will forgive our sins and cleanse us from all unrighteousness. (1 John 1:9)

HITTING AND FIGHTING

When I hurt another, bitter feelings arise that harm relationships and cause the person I hurt to sin too. Refusing to fight is the armor of a good and peaceful soul.

In the name of Jesus, I forgive

_____ *for* _____.

I pray for gentle hands and a
gentle tongue. Amen.

Let all bitterness and wrath and anger
and clamor and slander be put away
from you, with all malice, and be
kind to one another, tenderhearted,
forgiving one another, as God in Christ
forgave you. (Ephesians 4:31–32)

ACTING OUT MY ANGER

Losing one's temper is a selfish behavior used by those who feel out of control. Acting angry rarely has good results and damages relationships. I must stop and redirect myself when I feel anger coming.

Dear Jesus, teach me to reject anger and move away from the situation that made me angry, so I can calm down. Love,

He who is slow to anger has great understanding, but he who has a hasty temper exalts folly. (Proverbs 14:29)

MAKING A
WRONG CHOICE

God gave me a conscience to protect me from doing wrong. God gave me free will to choose right or wrong. Satan tries to encourage me do wrong, but I should choose to do right.

೧

Dear God, help me live uprightly by rejecting wrong. I belong to You. Love,

Be imitators of God, as beloved children. (Ephesians 5:1)

STEALING

Stealing is a crime. I should respect other people's property. I should not covet or steal from others but be content with what I have.

❧

Dear Jesus, I am sorry and will return or replace what I have taken. Please forgive me. Amen.

Let the thief no longer steal, but rather let him labor, doing honest work with his hands, so that he may be able to give to those in need. (Ephesians 4:28)

TAKING OTHERS' BELONGINGS WITHOUT PERMISSION

If I want to consume or use something that belongs to another, I must ask that person's permission. Taking is stealing and causes hard feelings. In rare instances, I could leave a note if I need to borrow something right away and should return it as soon as possible.

❧

Dear Jesus, give me ways to make amends to _____. Amen.

Treasures gained by wickedness do not profit, but righteousness delivers from death. (Proverbs 10:2)

EXCLUDING OTHERS

When I feel like excluding someone in a game or event, I should fight that feeling because it is from the devil. I wouldn't like to be treated that way.

Dear Jesus, I'm sorry that I made
_____ *feel bad.*
Please forgive me and show me
how to make this right. Amen.

When you give a feast, invite the poor,
the maimed, the lame, the blind, and
you will be blessed. (Luke 14:13)

BEING MEAN TO FAMILY PETS

Pets are part of our family, and they have feelings too. If I am nice to them, they will enjoy being around me. If I am mean to them, they will avoid me and might become aggressive.

Dear God, I'm sorry for hurting one of Your amazing creatures. Amen.

I know all the birds in the air, and all that moves in the field is mine. (Psalm 50:11)

TEASING

Teasing hurts others and causes hard feelings. Since I don't like being teased, I shouldn't tease others.

Dear God, help me to apologize and do something nice for _____ *to make up for being mean. Amen.*

Folly is a joy to him who has no sense, but a man of understanding walks aright. (Proverbs 15:21)

BULLYING

Bullying is mean and evil. God sees and hears ALL that I do to His creatures, so I must be careful not to offend Him.

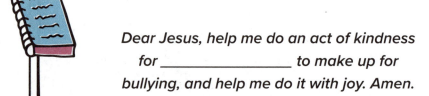

Dear Jesus, help me do an act of kindness for _____ to make up for bullying, and help me do it with joy. Amen.

See that you do not despise one of these little ones; for I tell you that in heaven their angels always behold the face of my Father who is in heaven. (Matthew 18:10)

BELITTLING OTHERS

I hurt someone today with insulting words. I know that the worst of me came out in those comments, and I need to repair what I said.

Dear Jesus, when I'm tempted to be unkind, help me to reject those evil words. Teach me to wear a cloak of self-control. Love,

God did not give us a spirit of timidity but a spirit of power and love and self-control. (2 Timothy 1:7)

DISRESPECTING AN ELDERLY PERSON

Elderly people might seem slow and fragile, but they are full of wisdom and experience, and they deserve honor and respect.

Dear God, please help me realize the beauty and wisdom of the aged so I can reach out to love them. I'm sorry for the disgraceful thing that I did. Amen.

You shall rise up before the [gray] head and honor the face of an old man, and you shall fear your God: I am the LORD. (Leviticus 19:32)

REJECTING CORRECTION

Every one of us has been corrected. That is how we learn and grow holier. I should not reject correction but must consider it as a gift that will help me become a better person.

Dear Jesus, console me. Forgive me. Help me mature. Amen.

A fool despises his father's instruction, but he who heeds admonition is prudent. (Proverbs 15:5)

REJECTING "NO" FOR AN ANSWER

When I'm told that I can't have or do something, it is because that thing is not good for me or the family budget won't allow it this week. I should not ask Mom for something that Dad has already said no to, and vice versa.

Dear God, help me to accept graciously each no. Amen.

Obey your leaders and submit to them; for they are keeping watch over your souls. (Hebrews 13:17)

SWEARING

Using foul words is a sin against those who hear them and a stain on my character. God's name is sacred and should NEVER be used irreverently.

Dear Jesus, I'm sorry for using foul words. Help me curb my tongue. Amen.

Let no evil talk come out of your mouths. (Ephesians 4:29)

SPENDING TOO MUCH TIME ON TECHNOLOGY

Science has shown that kids need to enjoy different types of activity. Playing games, sports, and doing crafts without technology develops my brain in alternate ways, helping me to be a better problem solver. |×

Dear Jesus, please help me reduce my technology use. Amen. ✗ 3

Do not be conformed to this world, but be transformed by the renewal of your mind, that you may prove what is the will of God, what is good and acceptable and perfect. (Romans 12:2)

USING UNACCEPTABLE APPS

If I cannot sit with my mother and use an app, it is not appropriate for me to use and must be deleted! Nor should I use inappropriate apps on my friends' devices. I should also unfriend people who post inappropriate content on social media.

❧

Dear Jesus, I am sorry for offending You by using inappropriate apps or reading inappropriate things. Please forgive me. Amen.

No temptation has overtaken you that is not common to man. God is faithful, and he will not let you be tempted beyond your strength, but with the temptation will also provide the way of escape, that you may be able to endure it. Therefore, my beloved, shun the worship of idols. (1 Corinthians 10:13–14)

LOOKING AT IMMORAL THINGS

I must protect my soul. My soul is the part of me where God dwells. Bad images and words hurt my soul.

Dear Jesus, please forgive me for_____. I renounce the improper things I saw and heard. Please help me to stop thinking about them. Amen.

Whatever is true, whatever is honorable, whatever is just, whatever is pure, whatever is lovely, whatever is gracious, if there is any excellence, if there is anything worthy of praise, think about these things. (Philippians 4:8)

LISTENING TO BAD MUSIC

Some people have put bad words to music. If I allow my mind to be fed bad words, I could start to think that bad things are good.

Dear Jesus, help me to make good choices in the music I listen to. Amen.

Take away from me the noise of your songs; to the melody of your harps I will not listen. But let justice roll down like waters, and righteousness like an ever-flowing stream. (Amos 5:23–24)

DISOBEYING MY PARENTS

Disobeying my parents directly breaks a commandment. I need to be ready to obey right away, even if I disagree with my parents. This pleases God and makes me virtuous.

O Lord, please help me to be obedient to my parents' decisions and to be kind in my tone of voice when I disagree with what I'm asked to do. Amen.

Children, obey your parents in the Lord, for this is right. (Ephesians 6:1)

BEING FRUSTRATED WITH MY PARENTS

When I become frustrated and reject what my parents teach and ask of me, I damage my relationship with them and with God.

O Lord, help me to accept my parents, be thankful for them, and show respect. Love,

"Honor your father and your mother, that your days may be long in the land." (Exodus 20:12)

TALKING BACK

Talking back is a poor character trait because it is rude and disrespectful. I must learn to hold my tongue.

Dear God, I am sorry for dishonoring those whom you set over me. Help me do something good to repair my relationship. Love,

A soft answer turns away wrath, but a harsh word stirs up anger. (Proverbs 15:1)

DISRESPECTING PHYSICAL BOUNDARIES

When my parents tell me that I must stay in the house, in the yard, or at a friend's house, I need to respect that boundary. If I go to a friend's house and then desire to go somewhere else, I must call my parents for permission. I understand that it is very important for my parents to keep me safe and know where I am.

Dear Jesus, please help me respect the boundaries set. Amen.

And he went down with them to Nazareth, and was obedient to them. (Luke 2:51)

NOT KEEPING MY WORD

When I tell someone in authority that I am going to do something, I need to do it! If I don't, two things happen: (1) I lose that person's trust; (2) I get a smudge on my character. If I cannot do what I promised, I must tell that person right away why I cannot do it.

❧

Dear Guardian Angel, please encourage me to do what I've promised to do. Love,

Let your yes be yes and your no be no, that you may not fall under condemnation. (James 5:12)

THE EXAMEN
FOR GROWING MY SOUL

St. Ignatius of Loyola taught a way to think about our day that has been used and taught since the 1500s. His method works so well to make a soul grow that everyone who wants to attain Heaven should practice these simple steps every day during a quiet time with God. Here's how to do it.

Dear God, please be with me as I think about my day.

Gratitude: Think of all the things you liked about today and give thanks to God!

Petition: Ask God for the grace to know what you did well and what you need to do better.

Dear God, please show me my sins and how You helped me today.

Review: Think about your day from morning till now—what you thought, what you said, and what you did.

Forgiveness: Tell God what you are sorry for, and ask Him to forgive your sins.

Thank the Lord that most of the time your children are trying to be good! This section is for children who have demonstrated that they are trying so hard that there is a little halo shining over them. While it may not be there all the time, they are truly trying and winning the battle most of the time. They deserve to be noticed in a special way. How your family rewards good behavior, whether it be their special day, a parent-child date, or a prize, is up to you.

In this section you will find a collection of Scripture verses and pages that you are welcome to photocopy to assist you in rewarding your saints in the making.

SHOWING LOVE AWARD

Dear _____,
sometimes you glow in such a way that
charity and love are the holy cloak that
you wear. You are therefore honored
with the **Showing Love Award** because
you work on what the Scriptures
say about love. Congratulations!

Love is patient and kind; love is not jealous or
boastful; it is not arrogant or rude. Love does not
insist on its own way; it is not irritable or resentful; it
does not rejoice at wrong, but rejoices in the right.
Love bears all things, believes all things, hopes all
things, endures all things. (1 Corinthians 13:4–7)

Beloved, let us love one another; for love
is of God, and he who loves is born of
God and knows God. (1 John 4:7)

Love covers a multitude of sins. (1 Peter 4:8)

GOOD WORKS AWARD

---

is recognized for so often going out of his or her way to do things for others with humility. Congratulations!

They are to do good, to be rich in good deeds, liberal and generous, thus laying up for themselves a good foundation for the future, so that they may take hold of the life which is life indeed. (1 Timothy 6:18–19)

But the fruit of the Spirit is love, joy, peace, patience, kindness, goodness, faithfulness, gentleness, self-control; against such there is no law. (Galatians 5:22–23)

Love your enemies and do good [to them]. (Luke 6:35)

SHOWING HOLINESS AWARD

_____, because
of the way that you have lived in the
truth of what you have learned through
faith, you have earned the Showing
Holiness Award. Congratulations!

Blessed are those whose way is blameless,
who walk in the law of the LORD!
Blessed are those who keep his testimonies,
who seek him with their whole heart. (Psalm 119:1–2)

Continue in what you have learned and
have firmly believed, knowing from whom
you learned it. (2 Timothy 3:14)

Ascribe to the LORD the glory due his name;
bring an offering, and come into his courts!
Worship the LORD in holy array;
tremble before him, all the earth! (Psalm 96:8–9)

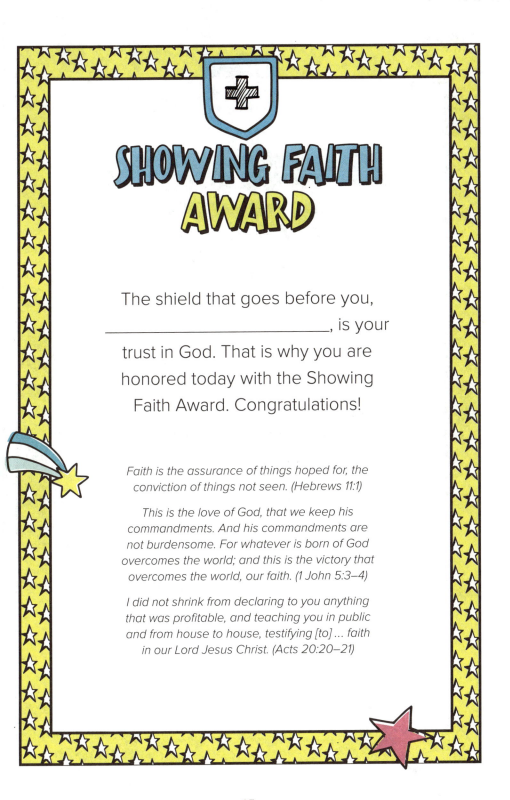

SHOWING FAITH AWARD

The shield that goes before you,

_____, is your

trust in God. That is why you are

honored today with the Showing

Faith Award. Congratulations!

Faith is the assurance of things hoped for, the conviction of things not seen. (Hebrews 11:1)

This is the love of God, that we keep his commandments. And his commandments are not burdensome. For whatever is born of God overcomes the world; and this is the victory that overcomes the world, our faith. (1 John 5:3–4)

I did not shrink from declaring to you anything that was profitable, and teaching you in public and from house to house, testifying [to] ... faith in our Lord Jesus Christ. (Acts 20:20–21)

DEMONSTRATING HUMILITY AWARD

Dear _____,
your little ways of being big in what the
Scriptures teach us to do and to be
have earned for you the Demonstrating
Humility Award. Congratulations!

Be kind to one another, tenderhearted,
forgiving one another, as God in Christ
forgave you. (Ephesians 4:32)

The fear of the LORD is instruction in wisdom, and
humility goes before honor. (Proverbs 15:33)

Blessed are the poor in spirit, for theirs is
the kingdom of heaven. (Matthew 5:3)

BEING A GOOD SUFFERER AWARD

_____,

your way of being happy with what you have or with what life deals you is to be praised. You are therefore honored with the Good Sufferer Award. Congratulations!

Keep your life free from love of money, and be content with what you have; for he has said, "I will never fail you nor forsake you." Hence we can confidently say, "The Lord is my helper, I will not be afraid; what can man do to me?" (Hebrews 13:5–6)

You also be patient. Establish your hearts, for the coming of the Lord is at hand. Do not grumble, brethren, against one another, that you may not be judged; behold, the Judge is standing at the doors. (James 5:8–9)

But when you fast, anoint your head and wash your face, that your fasting may not be seen by men but by your Father who is in secret; and your Father who sees in secret will reward you. (Matthew 6:17–18)

ABOUT
THE AUTHOR

Sally E. Follett was raised Lutheran and converted to Catholicism in 1984. She married her high school sweetheart after college, and while they desired children right away, they suffered infertility and miscarriages. After ten years, her motherhood was blessed by adoption, followed by three tummy babies.

Sally's career life began in marketing, and she used those skills to homeschool for nineteen years. She enjoys God's creation, being a mother and grandmother, tending her gardens, studying Scripture, entertaining, playing cards, and praying through all that life brings. Sally also contributes to her family business. She is a volunteer healing-prayer minister and is studying to be a spiritual director. Everything she does well she learned from books and the teachings of others, accepting these as gifts from God.

SOPHIA INSTITUTE

Sophia Institute is a nonprofit institution that seeks to nurture the spiritual, moral, and cultural life of souls and to spread the Gospel of Christ in conformity with the authentic teachings of the Roman Catholic Church.

Sophia Institute Press fulfills this mission by offering translations, reprints, and new publications that afford readers a rich source of the enduring wisdom of mankind.

Sophia Institute also operates the popular online resource CatholicExchange.com. *Catholic Exchange* provides world news from a Catholic perspective as well as daily devotionals and articles that will help readers to grow in holiness and live a life consistent with the teachings of the Church.

In 2013, Sophia Institute launched Sophia Institute for Teachers to renew and rebuild Catholic culture through service to Catholic education. With the goal of nurturing the spiritual, moral, and cultural life of souls, and an abiding respect for the role and work of teachers, we strive to provide materials and programs that are at once enlightening to the mind and ennobling to the heart; faithful and complete, as well as useful and practical.

Sophia Institute gratefully recognizes the Solidarity Association for preserving and encouraging the growth of our apostolate over the course of many years. Without their generous and timely support, this book would not be in your hands.

www.SophiaInstitute.com
www.CatholicExchange.com
www.SophiaInstituteforTeachers.org

Sophia Institute Press® is a registered trademark of Sophia Institute. Sophia Institute is a tax-exempt institution as defined by the Internal Revenue Code, Section 501(c)(3). Tax ID 22-2548708.